ribbon details

With projects and instructions for decorating with ribbons

mary norden

photography by sandra lane

RYLAND
PETERS
& SMALL

LONDON NEW YORK

First published in Great Britain
in 1999 as *Ribbons*
This revised edition published in
2002
by Ryland Peters & Small
Kirkman House
12–14 Whitfield Street
London W1T 2RP
www.rylandpeters.com

ISBN 1 900518 84 8
10 9 8 7 6 5 4 3 2 1

A catalogue record for this book is
available from the British Library

Publishing Director Anne Ryland
Designer Sally Powell
Editor Jo Lethaby
Editorial Manager
Sian Parkhouse
Production Alison Jones
Stylist Mary Norden
Additional photography
David Murray: 20, 40, 50, 58, 66,
88, 98, 132, 142-151
Jonathan Lovekin: 16–17, 117

Printed and bound in China

ribbon details

Most people traditionally associate ribbons only with gifts and bunches of flowers, but the almost overwhelming choice of ribbons now available means that it is possible to find one for every need, occasion and taste. The inspirational ideas and numerous projects in this book make use of a wide variety of different ribbon types, but by no means all, as well as showing the versatility of ribbon, which goes far beyond decorating Christmas presents and wedding bouquets.

The book is divided into three main creative sections, Ribbons in the Home, Ribbons for Festive Occasions and Ribbons and Flowers. The book finishes with a technical section, which includes a directory on types of ribbons used and step-by-step instructions on tying the different bows found throughout the book.

The first and largest section of the book illustrates the use of ribbons in the home – from enhancing soft furnishings and trimming bed and table linen to hanging and decorating pictures and mirrors. Any projects that involve sewing are kept very simple, requiring only the most basic of stitching, which can often be achieved without the use of a sewing machine, although it might take a little longer. Projects such as embellishing lampshades need no more than a pot of glue and others such as curtain tie-backs and some blankets, for example, require no additional materials – simply an attractive length of ribbon tied around or threaded through the fabric and finished with an exquisite bow.

The second section is full of ideas for making a festive occasion even more special by adding a touch of individual style. From original presentation of gifts and food to finishing touches for the table and decorating furniture and entire rooms, the ideas are certainly not intended only for Christmas but include any number of special events or celebrations

throughout the year – a spring wedding or a summer garden party, dinner parties, birthdays and anniversaries. Ideas can easily be adapted to suit any occasion simply by changing the type of ribbon or colour. For example, a table decorated with brightly coloured polka-dot ribbons is more suited to an alfresco meal, but for a winter dinner party by candlelight lengths of tartan ribbon would be more in keeping – especially for New Year's Eve or Burns Night. The success of all of these festive ideas, as with those in the rest of the book, depends on keeping it simple. A napkin rolled and tied with a plain bow has far more impact than one that is smothered in a complicated mass of ribbon; likewise, one single-coloured bow on the back of a chair with long tails that fall and flutter down towards the seat is far more effective than several stiff multi-coloured bows.

The third section of the book reinforces the pleasure of using ribbons with flowers – from the tiniest buttonholes and posies to ribbon-wrapped bouquets and vases and flowerpots. A bunch of flowers casually picked during an amble around the garden can be transformed into the realms of smart shopping with the right bow. Similarly, a little foliage from the hedgerow decorated with an interesting ribbon makes a far more striking and individual buttonhole than the traditional and rather predictable rose bud or carnation.

The aim of this book is not only to show how versatile and effective ribbons can be but also to inspire you, the reader, to create your own ideas and ways of using the many wonderful types of ribbon available.

Mary Norden

ribbons in
the home

Ribbons offer an easy way of adding style to your home, whether your theme is modern or traditional. Their most obvious use is with soft furnishings. Add single lengths of ribbon to the edges of curtains and to plain bed and table linen to make striking borders. Use ribbons tied into decorative bows to close pillow-cases and cushion covers instead of zips or buttons, or use a length of wide ribbon to tie back a curtain.

Other ideas for using ribbon around the home include using it to hang pictures and mirrors and to trim lamp-shades, shelf and table edges; and add a ribbon border to personalize a glass clip frame. Use ribbons to co-ordinate interiors, too: for example, in a sitting room use the same ribbon to trim the edge of a plain linen curtain and to trim the lampshade; in a pretty bedroom, use it to decorate the bed linen and as a curtain tie-back. As always, the possibilities are virtually endless.

bed linen
and blankets

There are many different ways of using ribbon to decorate bed linen and blankets, and with different results. For example, crisp white bed linen trimmed with straight lines of navy ribbon looks smart and dramatically different from that decorated with gathered and ruffled ribbons in soft feminine colours. For children there are pictorial ribbons with simple images of teddy bears, dolls and boats. Ribbons on bed linen can have practical uses, too. Ribbon ties, for example, can be used instead of buttons to fasten the openings of pillowcases and duvet covers.

For trimming bed linen you need a ribbon that is both washable and colourfast, while for decorating blankets, delicate ribbons that require dry cleaning, such as velvets, grosgrains and intricate jacquards woven with metallic

above right Plain and striped lilac ribbons are used to decorate three different pillowcases, which look lovely when mixed together on this wrought-iron bed.
below right A pretty sprigged pillowcase is edged with two rows of purple satin ribbon. Each length of ribbon is sewn on with just one row of stitching in matching thread.
far right The opening of a seersucker pillowcase is closed with pairs of lilac ribbon tied into bows. The ribbon was originally a wire-edge ribbon, but the wire was removed prior to sewing.

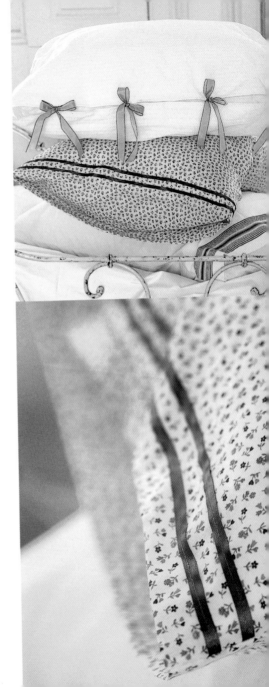

threads can also be used. Most woven-edge, and a few wire-edge, ribbons are washable – the wire in the latter needs removing by gentle pulling before using it for bed linen.

To secure the ribbon, stitch along either side of it as close to the edge as possible or, for very narrow ribbon, one row of stitching along the centre is sufficient. Alternatively, give the ribbon a slightly ruffled effect (see page 40) before sewing it on in a straight or wavy line.

If you are making your own bed linen and blankets the ribbon ends can be incorporated into the seam or hem allowances; otherwise you need to tuck under the raw ends before sewing the ribbon in place.

above left A pillowcase is closed with taffeta ribbon tied into bows.
below left An exquisite length of tiny flowers made of folded ombré ribbon is secured with hand stitching along the opening edge of a pillowcase.
right Three pillows demonstrate the different decorative options possible.

far left A pile of pressed plain sheets edged with ribbon demonstrates the use of various hard-wearing pictorial jacquard ribbons – a wonderful option for children's bed linen.

left A cotton jacquard ribbon woven with roses and edged with pink easily transforms a plain white sheet into pretty, feminine bed linen.

above The same sheet looks even more romantic when used on an old French day bed. The Oxford pillow-case is trimmed with red rickrack the same colour as the jacquard roses.

ribbon border bed cover

To make the lattice border for the 192 cm (76 in) long bed cover shown

here, you will need 4.20 m (4½ yd) of 1 cm (⅜ in) wide cotton ribbon in red

and 3.40 m (3¾ yd) of checked ribbon in the same width for each border.

one Mark out the position of the red ribbon on the bed cover using a tape measure

and pins. Position the two rows 5 cm (2 in) apart, with the first row 10 cm (4 in) from the

bottom edge of the cover. In each row place the first and the final pins about 2 cm (¾ in)

in from the side edges of the cover, with the other pins at 14.5 cm (5¾ in) intervals in between. Fold under the first 1 cm

(⅜ in) of the ribbon to hide the raw edge and pin the end onto the cover at the first pin.

Measure out 15.5 cm (6 in) of ribbon and pin this to the cover at the second pin position.

Repeat this process across the cover and for both rows of the border. Finish each row

with the ribbon ends turned under, as at the beginning of the row. The extra ribbon

between each pair of pins allows the two rows to be

tied together without distorting the cover. **two** Machine

stitch or hand sew the ribbon to the cover only at the points where the pins are

positioned. **three** Cut the checked ribbon into lengths of 25 cm (10 in). Slide these

under the two rows of red ribbon, positioning one halfway between each set of stitching;

tie each checked length into a simple bow, drawing the two rows of red ribbon together.

lift flap ▶

Extra wide satin ribbon is the traditional choice for hemming blankets. An alternative, however, is to use the narrowest satin ribbon and, using a blunt-ended tapestry or darning needle, thread it through loosely woven blanket fabric, such as mohair, to make border patterns. Choose ribbon no wider than 1 cm (⅜ in) otherwise it will distort both the ribbon and the blanket, and use a double-face ribbon if the ends are to be tied in a bow.

left Two cream blankets, one mohair, the other plain wool, are trimmed in different ways with satin ribbon. The narrower ribbon is laced through the loosely woven fabric while the wider ribbon is sewn along the edge of the other blanket to form a satin hem.
right Two rows of narrow satin ribbon have been laced through the blanket and the ribbon ends secured with a knot and a small neat bow at both ends of the laced border. This technique of lacing narrow ribbon could be repeated across the width of the blanket four or five times for a striped effect, if liked.

right A fine silk jacquard ribbon with a delicate paisley pattern in shades of grey adds a touch of luxury to an otherwise plain blanket. The blanket was made from a length of wide woollen fabric and the ribbon was sewn along only one side of the blanket. The other blanket is made from thicker wool and decorated with a narrow floral jacquard ribbon in black and beige.

far right Two Oxford pillowcases are finished with a stylish edging of ribbon. The wavy rickrack ribbon contrasts with the striped fabric of one pillow-case and the checked ribbon in black and beige adds pattern to the other plain pillowcase. Both the ribbons are made of cotton and are hard-wearing, which makes them an ideal choice for using on bed linen.

ribbons in the home

right and far right A Chinese silk
curtain is hung from a metal pole with
lengths of satin ribbon. Each ribbon
tie was evenly spaced along the top
edge of the curtain and stitched in
place before being threaded through
a curtain ring and tied in a bow.

above A plain cream curtain has
been given a stripy decorative
finishing touch with vertical rows of
narrow ribbon threaded through the
loosely woven curtain fabric.

curtains

Just as everyday bed linen can be turned into something special and individual with a length of ribbon and a few stitches so, too, can curtains. Since continual washing and general wear and tear is not such a consideration when choosing ribbons for curtains as it is for bed linen, the choice of ribbon type and the way in which it can be applied to a curtain is even greater – pleated satins, silk velvets, jacquards and picot-edge organdies can now all be used. Again, ribbons on curtains can be functional as well as decorative and one of the prettiest ways by which to hang a curtain is with lengths of ribbon tied into bows or even just simply knotted. The ribbon ends can either be trimmed short or left long so that they fall in with the folds of the curtain.

The curtain fabric and how you wish to decorate it will influence the choice of ribbon, particularly if a lot of sewing is involved. For example, if a long length of ribbon is to be sewn flat along the edge of a curtain to form a decorative border or hem, it must be of a suitable fabric. A jacquard or a satin ribbon would be appropriate for a velvet curtain because the fabrics are of a similar weight. A sheer ribbon, however, would be too delicate and would pucker during sewing.

Ribbon can be sewn in a single length along the edge of a curtain to form a border or several lengths can be arranged horizontally or vertically across the curtain fabric for a striped effect. If the fabric is loosely woven you could try weaving narrow ribbon through the fabric with a blunt-ended needle, as with the blankets earlier. Other patterns can be made by applying ribbon not as lengths but as ready-made single bows, which can be arranged in rows along one edge or scattered randomly across the curtain. Sew each bow into position by hand with a few backstitches. With fine curtain fabric, such as muslin or voile, leave the bow tails long so they flutter like butterflies when the window is open and the curtain moves in the breeze.

Alternative 'curtains' for windows and doors can be made simply by hanging lengths of ribbon. Use one

left and far left Lengths of rayon ribbon in pretty shades of pink, beige, silver grey and tan are tied into bows and then placed randomly across a fine cotton curtain. They are secured in position with a few hand stitches.

single type of ribbon or try an assortment in complementary colours, varying the length and width of the ribbons for extra interest. Tie or staple one end of each ribbon length to a wooden curtain pole and tie the other end to interesting objects such as glass baubles, or thread the end through shells, making holes if necessary with a hand drill. Different ribbon textures create different types of 'curtain': lengths of sheer ribbon will produce a romantic ethereal curtain as opposed to the more solid effect achieved with thicker non-translucent ribbon.

left A window is decorated with large clear glass baubles hung from pieces of ribbon. For this window dressing sheer ribbons only have been used and a simple bow in another ribbon in a complementary colour has been added to finish the top of each bauble.

above left and right As an alternative to a bauble and ribbon 'curtain', sea shells are tied on pieces of ribbon in a pretty assortment of aqua colours and of various widths and lengths. A mixture of ribbon types has also been used – plain and 'shot' organdie, cotton and rayon.

tie-backs

Tie-backs are usually crescent shaped and made of fabric which matches or contrasts with the curtain fabric. Although very neat, they often appear rather stiff and you might prefer instead to hold curtains back with casually tied lengths of ribbon. For this look to work you cannot be mean with the ribbon – use plenty of it so that after tying, the long ends can drape down among the curtain folds. A velvet curtain loosely tied back with a wide pleated ribbon looks wonderfully sumptuous like this,

and the ribbon has a habit of twisting gently as it falls. Alternatively, the ribbon can be tied into a bow. If you choose to use a sheer ribbon for a tie-back, give the bow more substance and interest by mixing two different, but complementary sheer ribbons.

The type of ribbon and tie-back is influenced by the style of the room and the curtain fabric. A kitchen curtain made from blue and white striped ticking looks best tied back with a simple plain blue cotton ribbon. A luxurious ribbon such as velvet or satin, or a complicated bow would be the wrong choice for the room and the type of fabric. In contrast, a romantic bedroom window dressed with a voile or muslin curtain looks wonderfully ethereal if tied back with another sheer – look out for exquisite appliquéd organdies and satin-edge georgette. On the other hand, a sitting room with vibrant coloured curtains would need something stronger, such as a wide striped ribbon in fluorescent colours or a print. Some of the best brightly coloured or patterned wide ribbons are wire-edge ribbons. These ribbons are ideal for moulding into elaborate bows and will hold their shape indefinitely, but if you prefer your tie-back to be more relaxed and floppy, simply remove the wire from the ribbon.

To make your tie-back more elaborate you could add a ribbon tassel (see page 66) or an extra bow to the first length of ribbon, or even a rosette bow (see page 150).

far left Ribbons offer an almost effortless way of tying back a curtain, particularly since there is little or no sewing involved. Here, a wide pleated taffeta ribbon with a wire edge and 'shot' with fluorescent pink and orange is tied casually so as to hold back a pink muslin curtain.

left A short length of old checked taffeta ribbon found in a junk shop was not quite long enough to make a tie-back, so was stitched on top of another slightly wider and much longer single-coloured taffeta ribbon. The finished ribbon was wrapped twice around the curtain before being tied into a bow, so that the checked pattern is clearly visible.

A printed voile curtain is pulled back with a wonderfully frothy bow of polka-dot organdie ribbon. The ribbon has been wrapped around the curtain and tied into a classic bow then another bow tied directly on top of the first one to form a type of double bow.

ruffled ribbon cushion

To calculate the amount of ribbon required for each ruffled stripe, measure the length of the chosen cushion cover fabric and multiply by 1½ to include gathering the ribbon and a seam allowance. For a fuller ruffle allow more ribbon per stripe. For the total amount of ribbon required for each cushion multiply this calculation by the number of stripes. When choosing your ribbon avoid thicker ribbon types such as velvets and grosgrains. The pale pink ribbon used here is 4 cm (1½ in) wide.

one Fold each length of ribbon in half lengthways and press lightly. This crease line marks the position of the gathering thread. Using thread in a contrasting colour, loosely stitch along the crease either by hand or using a

machine. Carefully gather the ribbon by pulling one end of thread. If you have used a sewing machine, pull the spool thread. **two** When the ribbon is ruffled to the required length, remembering to allowing a little extra for a seam allowance within the cushion cover, secure the thread ends with a knot or backstitches. Distribute the ruffles evenly

down the length of the ribbon then pin it in position on the fabric as shown. Using matching thread sew the ribbon onto the fabric with a line of machine or hand stitching worked as closely as possible to the gathering line. Finally, unpick the line of gathering stitches.

lift flap ▶

cushions
and bolsters

There are numerous ways in which ribbon can be used to turn a bland cushion or bolster that fades into the background into something special that gets noticed. One way is to apply ribbon as a border to emphasize the outline of the cushion. Simple ribbon trims can be added by hand to an existing cushion cover, while more flamboyant frills need to be incorporated into the seams when making up a cushion cover. Another technique is to use ribbons to create geometric patterns on an otherwise plain fabric – grids, stripes and diagonals are all possibilities. Mix different widths of ribbon as well as different patterns, but keep to the same type of ribbon texture. The ribbons can either be applied flat with one or two rows of machine stitching, or ruffled first and then sewn on to give a frilled effect across the cushion cover (see page 40). Lengths of ribbon can also be interlaced, using the simple principle of basket weaving, to create a striking cushion cover (see page 50). Use several colours for a draughtboard effect or just one colour to show off the weave better.

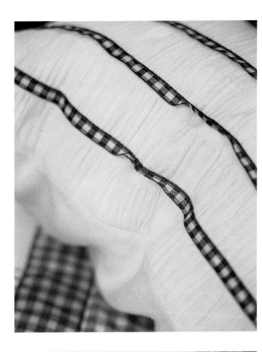

above right White seersucker has been decorated with lengths of narrow blue and white gingham ribbon before being made up into a cushion cover. Sewn along one long edge only, the ribbon gently ripples over the fabric.
right and far right Various blue and white ribbons are sewn onto cushion covers in bold geometric patterns.

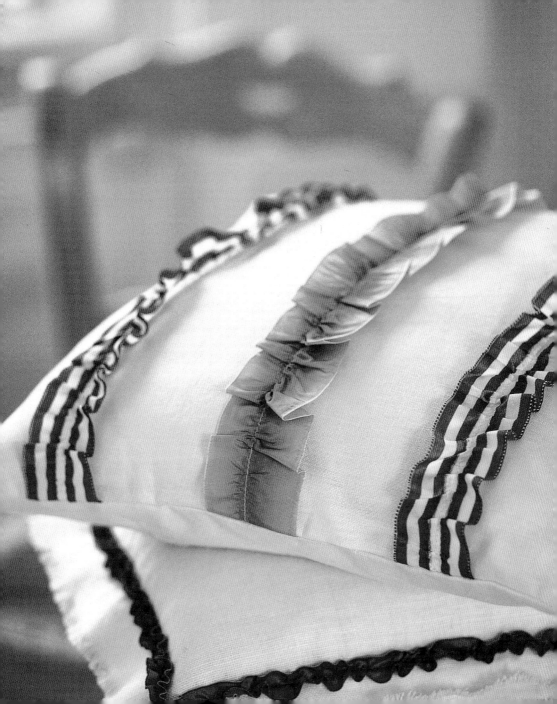

More ribbon ideas for cushions: a linen slip cover is closed with ties of checked ribbon and a narrow ruffled ribbon acts as a border.

Ribbons also make effective fastenings, and ribbon ties
are simpler than inserting zips or sewing on buttons for
closing a cushion or bolster cover. Bolsters in particular
have a tendency to look very formal and tailored so using
ribbon to close the ends gives a softer, more relaxed feel
as well as reducing the amount of sewing necessary.

left An exquisite iridescent moiré ribbon with dotted edges
is tied into simple bows to fasten each end of a silk bolster.

right A frilled double border made by layering satin and
organdie ribbons adds an extra touch of luxury to a
Chinese silk cushion. The two ribbons were tacked and then
gathered together along one edge to the required length,
then incorporated into the making up of the cushion cover.

below The front opening of a cushion is closed with a pair
of satin ribbons tied into a floppy bow.

ribbon weave cushion

The amount of ribbon required is determined by the ribbon width

and the area to be covered. To make this 35 cm (14 in) square

ribbon weave cushion front, you will need 7 m (7½ yd) of 4 cm

(1½ in) wide ribbon, plus a 38 cm (15 in) square of cotton fabric.

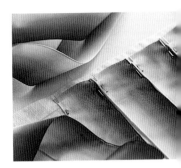

one Mark the cushion's 1.5 cm (½ in) seam allowance on the four edges of

the fabric, using a washable fabric marker. Cut the ribbon into 18 lengths of 38 cm (15 in). Pin half of the strips along

one edge of the fabric ensuring the ends are within the cushion's seam allowance and that there is no gap between the

strips. Machine stitch within 1.5 cm (½ in) of the edge of the fabric. Repeat along the opposite edge to secure the

ribbons. **two** Place the remaining strips over the secured ribbons at right angles, butting the first strip against the top

row of stitching and the last strip against the bottom row of stitching. Pin, then sew along one edge only, again within

the cushion's seam allowance, close to the first secured

strip but taking care not to catch it in the stitching.

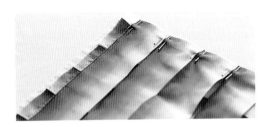

three Take the unstitched ribbon ends and weave them

alternately under and over the lower ribbons. Machine

stitch to secure, as before. Make up into a cushion cover.

lift flap ▶

lampshades

below left A plain lampshade has been decorated with lengths of a narrow picot-edge ombré ribbon arranged in stripes. Each stripe was glued in position, then finished with a tiny bow along the bottom edge. A clothes peg was used to hold the bows in place until the glue was dry.

below right Lengths of rayon ribbon give this lampshade its striped effect. Once the rayon was glued in place, a wired braid ribbon was attached top and bottom to neaten the edges and add an extra decorative touch.

right A plain lampshade was punched with holes through which an iridescent grosgrain ribbon was threaded and its ends secured with a bow.

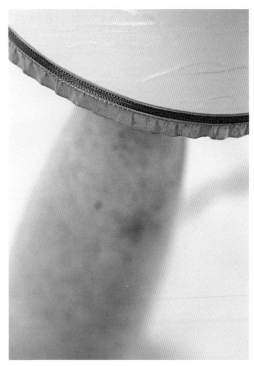

far left A striped lampshade with a twist: evenly spaced lengths of grosgrain ribbon were glued along the inside top edge of the shade. Once well stuck, the ribbon was twisted twice before being glued in position at the other end.

centre A cone-shaped lampshade is decorated with alternating stripes of rickrack and grosgrain in shades of lime green, turquoise and lilac for a fresh contemporary look.

left Ribbon comprising tiny coloured circles of coiled wired yarn is wound decoratively around a plain lampshade.

above A frill-edge taffeta ribbon in a contrasting colour finishes the edges of another lampshade.

ribbon-bound lampshade

The size of the shade and the degree to which it slopes determine the amount of ribbon required.

For a rough calculation, wind a length of string around one-quarter of the frame. Space it along the

bottom ring slightly closer than the width of the ribbon to be used, and even closer together along

the top ring to allow for overlap and the slope of the shade (unless it is

straight). For the total amount of ribbon required, multiply the length of

string used by four, adding an extra 5 cm (2 in) for starting and finishing.

one Starting inside the bottom ring of the frame, fold 2.5 cm (1 in) of one ribbon end

over and around the ring. Stick firmly in place with a little multi-purpose glue. If neces-

sary, secure with a clothes peg until the glue is dry. **two** With the ribbon

facing out and kept taut, bring it up the outside of the frame, over the top ring

and back down inside to overlap the start slightly. Continue wrapping tightly

in this way. The ribbon will need to overlap

slightly more at the top of the shade than at the

bottom to account for any slope. If you run out of ribbon, neatly glue or stitch a second

length to the first, inside the shade near the bottom or top. **three** When the frame is

covered, secure the ribbon end with glue on the inside, or on the outside at the bottom

if it will be covered by braid. Glue braid in position and secure with clothes pegs until dry.

lift flap ▶

photo frames and pictures

Decorating plain photo frames with lengths of ribbon is a far more innovative and creative option than simply slipping the picture into a ready-made frame. Unless the glass needs to be cut specially to fit the picture, inexpensive clip frames are ideal for using in this way.

If necessary, first cover the picture mount with paper – off-white or cream is better than brilliant white paper and, if possible, use paper that has some texture. Position the picture on the mount and secure it in place with a little multi-purpose glue or double-sided tape. Place the glass on top and bind the edges of the mount and glass together with masking tape, making sure the tape over-laps the front of the frame by less than the width of the ribbon to be used. Cut four strips of ribbon to fit the edges of the frame, allowing a little extra for wrapping over the frame edge to the back. Keeping the ribbon taut, fix the strips along the top and bottom edges first, before positioning the two remaining strips on the sides. For small pictures a dab of glue at each corner, front and back, is usually enough. For larger pictures a little glue along the edges of the strips of ribbon will be necessary, but be careful not to apply too much glue otherwise you might spoil the ribbon. It is best to test the ribbon before-hand to see how well it will take the glue. Hold the ribbon in place with a clothes peg until the glue is dry.

Hard-wearing grosgrain ribbon is ideal for covering shades, and different effects are possible with ombré ribbon, which gradually shades from dark to light, according to whether you overlap the dark or the paler edge as you wind it around the lampshade.

left and far left A group of family photographs is framed with different but co-ordinating ribbons – a suede ribbon, a striped ribbon made of paper and a wider striped satin sheer, all in sophisticated shades of brown. For framing pictures choose suitable ribbons such as grosgrain, woven jacquard and satin, which have more stability and strength than delicate single sheers. Not only are sheers too fragile on their own but their translucent quality is completely lost when glued down.

right A collection of old postcards is grouped together vertically, running down a length of blue satin ribbon, which is cut into an inverted 'V' shape at the bottom and finished at the top with a floppy bow.

left Larger pictures and mirrors, like this one framed in painted bamboo, look good hung with ribbon, especially if you want to make more of a feature of them. If they are very heavy, hang them with wire or string then hide the wire with a long length of ribbon, such as the wide lilac satin used here, and finish the ribbon with a simple bow.

below A group of botanical prints are hung individually from lengths of gold iridescent grosgrain and arranged along the wall in a row.

Hanging cards with ribbon is usually something done only at Christmas, which is a shame since it is a wonderful way of displaying pictures and photographs that might otherwise be left in a drawer or a pile. Using ribbon in this way also allows you to decorate your home with an interesting and personal touch. The arrangement of pictures can either be horizontal in which case each picture is hung from its own length of ribbon, or in a long vertical row with all the pictures on the same ribbon. Secure your pictures to the ribbon with double-sided tape and attach the top of the ribbon to the wall with a picture pin or small nail, which can then be concealed by a small bow if wished.

tassels

Tassels are incredibly easy and quick to make. Almost any type of narrow ribbon can be used. The length of the tassel depends on the size of the piece of cardboard used, and its thickness on the number of times you wind the ribbon around it – the more ribbon you use, the fuller the tassel will be. For the tassel shown here, you need about 2.5 m (2¾ yd) of 3 mm (⅛ in) wide satin ribbon, plus 25 cm (10 in) of slightly wider ribbon in a contrasting colour for attaching the tassel to the key.

one Cut a piece of cardboard 8 cm (3 in) wide. Holding one end of the ribbon against the card to begin, wind all of the ribbon around the card. Do not allow the ribbon to twist. **two** Slip the length of contrasting ribbon under all the strands on the cardboard and knot it firmly at the top of the cardboard as shown, leaving the ends long. These ends are used to tie the tassel to the key.

three Slide the tassel off the cardboard. Wind a small length of satin ribbon (in a matching or a contrasting colour) around the tassel, about 1 cm (⅜ in) from the top; knot firmly. Trim the ends and tuck them underneath or secure with a few stitches.

l i f t   f l a p ▶

napkins, mats and tablecloths

For decorating table linen always select the ribbons with care. Consider how the linen is going to be used and how often. For example, a napkin or tablecloth that might be used on a regular basis should be trimmed with a hard-wearing washable ribbon such as a checked cotton or a rickrack, while a delicate napkin made of voile and used only for special occasions could be decorated with something more dainty, like an intricately worked braid or a narrow jacquard ribbon.

Ribbon tassels add opulence to curtain tie-backs, table corners, the backs of bridal chairs and even door handles, while tiny tassels can be tied to keys, gifts and rolled napkins as a finishing touch.

far left A narrow grosgrain ribbon edged with running stitches in cream adds interest to a plain maroon napkin and gives it a smart look.

centre left top A delicate braid enlivens the edges of a cotton napkin.

centre left bottom A braided ribbon has been hand sewn onto a translucent voile napkin in a diagonal cross, using tiny running stitches and the occasional backstitch.

left For a neat finish on this linen napkin with a frayed edge, the ribbon trim has been folded into a diagonal pleat at each corner before sewing.

A cheerful mix of table mats trimmed with one or two rows of rickrack, together with a napkin tied with ribbon in complementary bright sunny colours, looks effective on a white tablecloth.

ribbons in the home

For sets of co-ordinating table linen, try using the same patterned ribbon in different widths: trim a tablecloth with a wide checked ribbon and the napkins with a narrower version. Alternatively, a narrow ribbon on a napkin or mat could be applied in several rows along a tablecloth to look like a wide ribbon border.

Experiment with different ways of arranging the ribbon, too. Appliqué two lengths of ribbon across table linen, either diagonally or horizontally and vertically, to form a striking cross. Place two or three rows of ribbon on either side of a table mat rather than all the way around. Or try layering ribbons – a rickrack on top of a wider ribbon with straight edges, for example – and if the linen has a drawn threadwork border, lace narrow ribbon through the fabric.

right A red grosgrain ribbon embroidered with cream contrasts smartly with a blue jute table mat.
far right Trim a set of mats with different but co-ordinating ribbons rather than have them all identical.

Two different ribbons, a plain cotton and a narrow
ombré with a picot edge, have been appliquéd
onto a pale blue tablecloth in a simple grid
pattern. To complement the tablecloth, surplus
ribbon is tied together into a bow around the
neck of a small glass vase.

ribbons for
festive occasions

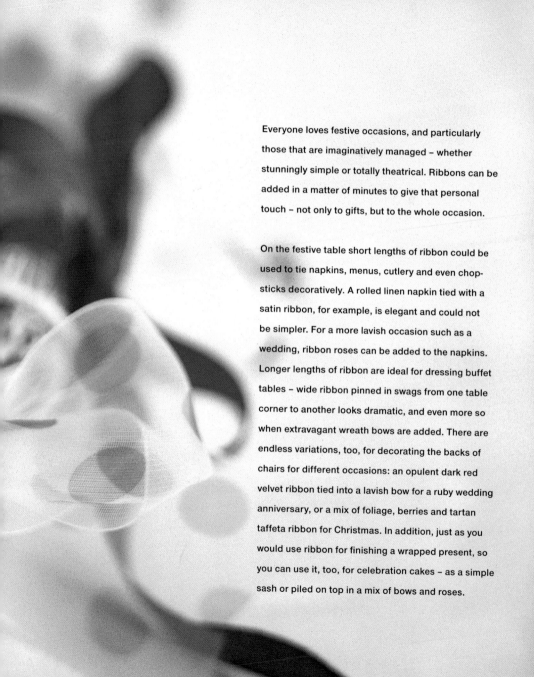

Everyone loves festive occasions, and particularly those that are imaginatively managed – whether stunningly simple or totally theatrical. Ribbons can be added in a matter of minutes to give that personal touch – not only to gifts, but to the whole occasion.

On the festive table short lengths of ribbon could be used to tie napkins, menus, cutlery and even chopsticks decoratively. A rolled linen napkin tied with a satin ribbon, for example, is elegant and could not be simpler. For a more lavish occasion such as a wedding, ribbon roses can be added to the napkins. Longer lengths of ribbon are ideal for dressing buffet tables – wide ribbon pinned in swags from one table corner to another looks dramatic, and even more so when extravagant wreath bows are added. There are endless variations, too, for decorating the backs of chairs for different occasions: an opulent dark red velvet ribbon tied into a lavish bow for a ruby wedding anniversary, or a mix of foliage, berries and tartan taffeta ribbon for Christmas. In addition, just as you would use ribbon for finishing a wrapped present, so you can use it, too, for celebration cakes – as a simple sash or piled on top in a mix of bows and roses.

left A place card is tied to the stem of a sweet pea with moiré taffeta ribbon and placed on a napkin.

above right Tiny bows in striped grosgrain complete these place cards.

below right Rolled menus are tied with organdie and placed in wine glasses.

far right An invitation is attached to a chair back by a narrow taffeta ribbon

finishing touches

It is often the smallest details at a party table, whether it is for a large smart wedding or an informal dinner for four, that make the most impact and thus turn it into a memorable occasion. However simple, such finishing touches add a sense of individual style.

The success of these details depends on using appropriate ribbons in a way that best complements the occasion. For Christmas and winter weddings velvet ribbons in deep opulent colours and taffeta in traditional plaids are the perfect partners for white damask table linen, while for summer and outdoor occasions use organdies, which make romantic-looking bows and shimmer in the light.

When choosing ribbons to finish your table also consider if any, the flowers. The ribbons should complement the flowers and the way in which they are presented, not only in colour but also in texture. A navy and cream jacquard ribbon or a pleated velvet, for example, would be too smart and heavy used on the same table as an informal bowl of freshly picked sweet peas.

For the prettiest table settings decorate menus and place cards with tiny bows secured with double-sided tape or a dab of glue. Punch holes in menus and invitations and thread with ribbon to hang from the backs of chairs. The possibilities are as endless as the choice of ribbons.

left Pairs of chopsticks are elegantly tied with short lengths of cream satin and checked ribbon. The silky texture of the satin and the choice of colour contrasts well with the matt black chopsticks **right** For a buffet, satin ribbon in sophisticated shades of pale coffee, gre and cream is used to tie cutlery wrapped in thick white napkins.

Use ribbons instead of napkin rings to secure rolled napkins. Choose the ribbon to fit the occasion: try brightly striped and patterned ribbons for a summer party, satin and sheers for a wedding or velvet for an extravagant dinner. Experiment with different ways of tying the napkin, as well as adding flowers and foliage. Another option is to tie ribbons around cutlery, or decorate the handle of a wedding cake knife with a long ribbon of iridescent organdie or taffeta, leaving the bow tails long so they drape and shimmer across the table.

top Ribbon tied around a rolled napkin makes an alternative napkin ring.
above A napkin folded into a square, rather than rolled, is gathered up and secured with a ribbon to match.

ribbon roses

The simplest ribbon roses are made from just one continuous strip of wire-edge ribbon and there is

no sewing involved, which makes them incredibly quick to make. A more elaborate double rose can

be made using two different coloured ribbons: two shades of pink, for example. Simply knot the two

ribbons together at one end and proceed as

for a single rose, ruffling and winding the two

ribbons together. For each single rose you will

need 1 m (1¼ yd) of wire-edge ribbon.

one Tie a knot in the ribbon as close as possible to one

end. At the opposite end, pull out the wire along one edge, so that the ribbon starts to ruffle. **two** As you continue

pull the wire with one hand, gently tease the ribbon back towards the knot with the other hand. Pull until the length

ribbon is completely gathered. **three** Holding the knotted end in one han

coil the gathered edge around the knot. Wind the remaining wire around th

knot several times to secure. Gently tease out

the ungathered edge of the ribbon so that the

'rose' looks more like a bloom than a tight bud.

The excess wire can be trimmed or used to

secure the flower to the napkin, as here.

l i f t   f l a p

left Pairs of chopsticks are elegantly tied with short lengths of cream satin and checked ribbon. The silky texture of the satin and the choice of colour contrasts well with the matt black chopsticks. **right** For a buffet, satin ribbon in sophisticated shades of pale coffee, grey and cream is used to tie cutlery wrapped in thick white napkins.

Use ribbons instead of napkin rings to secure rolled napkins. Choose the ribbon to fit the occasion: try brightly striped and patterned ribbons for a summer party, satin and sheers for a wedding or velvet for an extravagant dinner. Experiment with different ways of tying the napkin, as well as adding flowers and foliage. Another option is to tie ribbons around cutlery, or decorate the handle of a wedding cake knife with a long ribbon of iridescent organdie or taffeta, leaving the bow tails long so they drape and shimmer across the table.

top Ribbon tied around a rolled napkin makes an alternative napkin ring.
above A napkin folded into a square, rather than rolled, is gathered up and secured with a ribbon to match.

ribbon roses

The simplest ribbon roses are made from just one continuous strip of wire-edge ribbon and there is no sewing involved, which makes them incredibly quick to make. A more elaborate double rose can be made using two different coloured ribbons: two shades of pink, for example. Simply knot the two ribbons together at one end and proceed as for a single rose, ruffling and winding the two ribbons together. For each single rose you will need 1 m (1¼ yd) of wire-edge ribbon.

one Tie a knot in the ribbon as close as possible to one end. At the opposite end, pull out the wire along one edge, so that the ribbon starts to ruffle. **two** As you continue pull the wire with one hand, gently tease the ribbon back towards the knot with the other hand. Pull until the length

ribbon is completely gathered. **three** Holding the knotted end in one han coil the gathered edge around the knot. Wind the remaining wire around t

knot several times to secure. Gently tease out

the ungathered edge of the ribbon so that the

'rose' looks more like a bloom than a tight bud.

The excess wire can be trimmed or used to

secure the flower to the napkin, as here.

lift flap

An exquisite ribbon rose framed by a floppy bow and tails in burgundy organdie ribbon decorates the corner of a table draped in crisp white linen.

ribbons for festive occasions

right A rosette in checked wire-edge ribbon finished with a co-ordinating silky bow makes a wonderful corner decoration on a table set for a special occasion. The bow tails have been left extra long so as to fall within the folds of the tablecloth.

far right Two lengths of ribbon, one diaphanous with a picot edge and the other satin, are looped and tied together in a simple bow and then pinned to the corner of a tablecloth for an incredibly easy yet effective decoration. The picot edge of the organdie ribbon picks up the eyelet detail of the white tablecloth.

tables and chairs

There are times when simply covering a table with a cloth is not quite effective enough for a special occasion, particularly when the table is to take centre stage. A buffet table laden with food and flowers can look bare at the corners and sides because it is not surrounded by chairs. Similarly, a table intended for the wedding cake might need a little more decoration to emphasis its importance. For simplicity and speed ribbons can simply be laid across a table like narrow runners and allowed to hang over the sides, or long lengths can be pinned from one corner to another in generous swags. Table corners look wonderful dressed with extravagant wreath bows or rosettes secured in place with long-tailed bows. Alternatively, place one tablecloth on top of another and gather up the top cloth at each corner with a bow to create opulent folds of fabric and reveal the contrasting cloth underneath.

left Lengths of brightly coloured ribbon printed with white polka dots are casually placed across a table set for an alfresco meal. The varying lengths of ribbon and the two different widths add to the informality of the occasion.

below and right Add drama to a summer buffet table with ribbons in bright fluorescent colours. First pin a swag of shocking pink taffeta ribbon from one corner to another, choosing a woven rather than a wire-edge ribbon so that it will drape well across the cloth. Make single bows using the same ribbon and attach one to each corner, leaving the bow tails long. Make double bows from a contrasting ribbon with wire edges, which will allow you to mould the loops of each bow into a full puffed-out shape. Pin these to each corner, on top of the single bows, to complete the decoration.

wreath bows

A wreath bow consists of two contrasting ribbons twisted into loops and then tied together to create

a wonderful froth of looping ribbon with long tails. You will need 2.5 m (2¾ yd) of each ribbon, plus

15.5 cm (6 in) of narrow ribbon or florist's wire.

one Set aside 50 cm (20 in) of each ribbon. Place one

ribbon horizontally in front of you on a flat surface. Fold

the ribbon 18 cm (7 in) from the right-hand edge to form

the first loop; return it to the centre and twist it over. Fold the ribbon another 18 cm (7 in), to form a second loop and the

return the ribbon to the left, twisting it at the centre as before. **two** Repeat this process until you have four loops e

either side of the centre and the ends of the ribbon fini

up on opposite sides. Secure with a clothes peg wh

you fold and loop the contrasting ribbon in the same wa

three Place one bow on top of the other and tie the

together in the centre with the narrow ribbon or wire. W

one reserved ribbon length on top of the other, place

them under the bow. Tie them in a single knot around the

centre of the bow to hide the wire or narrow ribbon and

form long tails. Fluff up the bow, fanning out all the loops.

lift flap

This cake is strikingly but very simply decorate
with a sash made from two contrasting ribbons
length of wide pleated orange taffeta is wrapp
around the cake and topped with a narrower
black and white ribbon with a picot edge.

celebration cakes

left A pink wire-edge ribbon has been passed beneath an iced cake and tied into a bow on top. A single bow in a contrasting colour is added for an extravagant finish.

below left An exquisite floral braided ribbon is arranged in swags around an iced cake and pinned in position. Small grosgrain bows in matching vibrant blue with red edging have been added to the top of the swags.

below For this sophisticated centrepiece a cake is dressed with a sash of silk and topped with a ribbon rose and bow.

special presentation

As with most of the ideas in this book, the decorating of gifts or other items with ribbon requires no special skills or tools – just a little care, thought and imagination. However simply applied, ribbon can transform a quite ordinary object into something special, as long as it always enhances the item and does not smother it.

The different colours and textures of ribbon and the manner in which it is applied determines the different effects possible. A gift wrapped in white tissue paper, tie with a shimmering pastel-coloured organdie and finishe in a bow with long trailing tails, has a soft feminine look. The same gift would look quite different, however, if it w decorated with a smart navy grosgrain ribbon, knotted tied in a small neat bow.

above left Old-fashioned tiny sweet boxes made from thin white card are closed with silky ribbon cord and displayed on a glass cake stand.
below left Cones overflowing with Easter treats are decorated with criss-crossed remnants of silk ribbon topped with a bow of narrow organdie ribbon.
right Duck's eggs for an Easter display are trimmed with an assortment of narrow ribbons. It is best to secure the ribbon at one end of each egg first by glueing it in positi before tying the ribbon into a bow at the other end.

far left A large present wrapped in handmade Japanese paper is decorated with different but complementary diaphanous ribbons – a narrow organdie ribbon placed over a wider ribbon of satin-edge georgette.

left Homemade cookies have been stacked into piles then wrapped in clear cellophane and secured with an elastic band. They are decorated with ribbon tied into a simple bow only at the top, or wrapped around the whole gift and finished with a bow.

ribbons for festive occasions

When choosing ribbon always consider the size of the item to be decorated since you do not want to swamp it with too much ribbon; similarly, too narrow a ribbon on a large object will look out of proportion and mean. Other factors to consider are the 'feel' you wish to convey. For a traditional Christmas look the obvious ribbons are metallics in gold, taffeta in red and green plaids, and deep, richly coloured velvets; while for a more flamboyant look, wire-edge ribbons in vibrant turquoises and purples are more appropriate.

The colour and texture of the wrapped gift or the surface of the object to be decorated should also be considered. For a contrast of textures team a silky satin ribbon with a heavily textured handmade paper, or a picot-edge organdie with a shiny cellophane wrap. Or experiment with contrasts of colour and pattern: a fine jacquard ribbon wrapped around a bowl with cracked glazing, or a duck's egg trimmed with a georgette ribbon.

Using two different ribbons together offers other possibilities. You could try pairing up plain and patterned ribbons of the same or of differing widths for various effects. For example, team a pale blue cotton tape with a blue and white gingham, or perhaps a black silk with a black and yellow polka dot.

left The top of a wooden bucket is decorated with a gingham swag and neat bows in a contrasting ribbon before being used to hold napkins at a buffet party.

Not all presents need be hidden in wrapping paper. These Japanese bowls, some filled with sweets, are simply tied with different ribbons – a picot- and satin edge sheer, a picot-edge grosgrain and a checked satin.

addition to presents, containers
uch as baskets, vases and cake
tands all benefit from a decoration
f ribbon. It might be as simple a
ick as tying a taffeta bow to the
andle of a pewter jug, weaving a
rosgrain ribbon around the top of
basket or trimming the rim of a
ooden bowl with small bows. If the
ecoration is to be only temporary
ecure the ribbon with double-sided
pe or, for permanence, use dabs
strong multi-purpose glue. The
ing to remember is not to overdo
e decoration. A glass bowl, for
ample, would look far more
amatic adorned with a single satin
w than with a highly patterned
bon tied in a complicated bow.
ways resist the temptation of
ing too much ribbon, however
autiful it might be.

t A stack of wrapped soap is
d together and then finished with
mart matching pleated bow.
ht Small bottles of bath oil are
pped in lilac organza and finished
h two different ribbons combined
ether into one simple bow.

festive decorations

A bare room or an unadorned Christmas tree can be quickly transformed with just a few lengths of ribbon. Use short lengths, perhaps remnants from another ribbon project or leftover from gift wrapping, to decorate plain Christmas baubles. Carefully remove each bauble's metal neck piece and wire loop before decorating. Secure the lengths of ribbon at the base and around the neck of the bauble with either strong glue or, if only temporary, with double-sided tape. When the neck piece is replaced it should cover the ribbon ends. For elegant simplicity all the baubles could be decorated with just one type of ribbon – a red bauble trimmed with tartan or metallic grosgrain ribbon for example – or you might prefer a co-ordinated mixture: polka dots, checks and stripes in black and white around silver baubles.

left These Christmas baubles are decorated with ribbon and hung as a group, then crowned with a length of stripe ribbon folded into floppy loops. Decorating plain baubles in this way is an excellent way of using up all those small pieces of exquisite ribbon you cannot bear to throw away

right Simple white candles look sophisticated when tied into a pile with two contrasting ribbons – a wide diaphane organdie is offset by a narrower ribbon of turquoise grosgrain edged in lime green. The bow tails of the latter have been deliberately left long to trail over the table.

Use ribbon, too, instead of wire or cord, to hang tree decorations. Alternatively, decorate your Christmas tree with just single or double bows. Choose rich burgundy and purple satins or velvets for a sumptuous look, gold or silver metallic ribbons for a glitzy effect, or jutes, cottons and ginghams in red for a natural Scandinavian look. Crown the tree with one spectacular bow to finish.

far left A sumptuous satin bow decorates a candle holder.

left Glass drops, remnants of a broken chandelier, are tied with ribbons of various widths to make tree decorations.

above As an alternative to the traditional Christmas tree, a branch is hung with starfish on lengths of pale ribbon.

Ribbons to decorate the home work best when used boldly and simply. Tie bows to chandeliers, leaving the tails long to flutter gently and shimmer in the light. Add trailing bows to the base of candlesticks and vases. Fix bows to the tops of mirrors and pictures and, on an even larger scale, decorate fireplaces, tables, staircases and doors with swathes of ribbon.

above and right A mantelpiece, hung with pleated orange taffeta ribbon and picture bows in checked ribbon, is the focal point for a festive room. The taffeta is twisted as it is arranged in loops and held in position with double-sided tape. The picture bows can be taped or pinned on top.

ribbon
wreaths

left and far left A twig wreath has
been lightly sprayed with white paint
and decorated with six bows in a
sheer ribbon, on top of which are
smaller contrasting bows in narrow
gingham and taffeta edged with satin.

**overleaf left, clockwise from top
left** A wreath base covered with wide
metallic ribbon and decorated with
gold bows makes an alternative to
the traditional Christmas wreath of
berries and foliage.

A length of pleated wire-edge ribbon
forms a scalloped wreath when it is
pinched at regular intervals and
tied to a circular wire frame with
contrasting ribbon.

A door knob is decorated with a
wreath hung from a loop of red
and cream checked taffeta ribbon.

A wedding wreath is covered with
ribbon roses and simple bows.

overleaf, right In keeping with
its delicate quality, this wreath of
dried leaves has been hung by a
diaphanous satin-edge ribbon.

ribbons and flowers

Ribbons are particularly effective when used with flowers. A length of ribbon casually tied into a simple bow is all that is required to turn a simple bunch of garden flowers into something special. A tiny posy of violets needs no more than a plush velvet ribbon to become exquisite, while a mix of cow parsley, sweet peas and other summer flowers is delightful when tied with a froth of shimmering organdie. Different effects can be achieved, according to the type of ribbon used and the way in which it is applied. A bouquet of pale-coloured roses bound and finished with a thick satin ribbon will look luxurious and suitable for a smart wedding, while the same flowers tied with a pretty gingham bow will look more relaxed and informal.

Ribbons may also be used to decorate vases, jugs or pots of flowers and work well with single flowers and buds to produce some stunning buttonholes.

posies

far left A bunch of old-fashioned aquilegias is held with two different but complementary ribbons tied in a simple bow.

above left A tiny posy of sweetly scented lily of the valley is tied with a frothing bow of almost translucent ribbon decorated with tiny dots.

below left Lilac and sweet peas are decorated with a wide lilac velvet ribbon.

above The choice of a velvet ribbon for this exquisite posy has been dictated by the velvety petals and colours of the violas.

ribbon-wrapped bouquet

Wrapping the stems of a bouquet with ribbon is done for both

decorative and practical reasons, particularly for a wedding bou-

quet which will probably be held for a long time. To bind a small

bouquet you will need 1 m (1¼ yd) of 2.5 cm (1 in) wide satin

ribbon, plus florist's wire or string and tape or multi-purpose glue.

one Using string, florist's wire or narrow ribbon tie the flower stems together

at both ends. Trim all the stem ends to the same length. Cut the length of satin

ribbon in half. Take one length and wrap one end at an angle around the base of the stems as shown. Bring the ribb

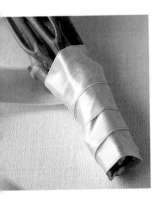

around, close to the cut stem ends and over the ribbon end to secure it in positic

two Continue to wrap the ribbon around the stems, keeping the ribbon taut a

ensuring that each overlap is evenly spaced

and at the same angle. When the stems are

completely covered, cut the excess ribbon and

secure the end of the wrapped ribbon with

either tape or a small dab of glue. **three** Place the second length of ribbon

under the stems at the end of the wrapped ribbon. Tie a simple bow over the

top of the wrapped ribbon to help secure it and to finish off the bouquet.

lift flap

uttonholes

ating attractive buttonholes for lapels offers enormous
be and fun for combining flowers, foliage and ribbons
variety of different effects.

ding favourites can be presented in completely
nal ways: for example a classic red rose finished with
k and white gingham ribbon, or an ivy paired with a
ed silk. The choice of flower or foliage, and the way
hich it is decorated should reflect the feel of the
sion. For a formal wedding, a rose or tulip bud
itifully dressed with a satin ribbon is suitable, while a
delphinium finished with a blue and white checked
is perfect for a summer country wedding and a burnt
ge dahlia tied with a ruby red grosgrain is flamboyant.
effect is all in the detail, however simple it is.

des suiting the style of the wedding, buttonholes can
important part of an outfit. For example the groom's
nhole should enhance as well as co-ordinate with
of his attire, such as his tie or waistcoat. With this in
, do not mix pattern with pattern. A spray of pretty
e tied with a floral jacquard ribbon woven in greens,
ws and oranges looks far better with a plain mustard-
red waistcoat than with a brocade one or with a
ked tie. Instead, team these with a plain ribbon that
up one of the colours in the pattern and perhaps
match the fabric used, pairing a silk ribbon with a
e for example.

above Buttonholes do not necessarily have to consist of a traditional flower, such as a rose or a carnation, formally paired with a shiny satin ribbon. Try using unusual flowers and distinctive foliage instead. For this more casual look, tie a narrow picot-edge ribbon around a small sprig of foliage in a classic 'shoelace'-style bow, or match the distinctive small lime green flowers of lady's mantle with a finely striped silk ribbon.

right A bright orange gerbera appears even more flamboyant when tied with a length of turquoise grosgrain ribbon edged with lime green. This softer textured grosgrain can be tied in a bow, unlike some of the stiffer versions.

far right Experiment with ribbon width, size of bow and colour when creating buttonholes. Black and white gingham is effective here with fresh green colours.

left Cream grosgrain ribbon with a picot edge is used to decorate a galvanized bucket with stripes, making it a perfect table centrepiece

below The handle of an enamelled water jug of flowers is decorated with a diaphanous pale blue ribbon tied into a large floppy bow.

ases and flowerpots

uquets and pots of flowers presented as gifts are often
corated with a bow and after they are unwrapped it is a
me not to make the most of the ribbon. Use it by tying
asually into a loose bow around the vase neck or onto
handle. Alternatively, using a good multi-purpose glue,
ch stripes of ribbon onto the surface of a container to
ke a decorative grid or striped pattern. Thicker ribbons
h as grosgrains and woven jacquards are particularly
ed for this type of decoration, adding not only colour
pattern but also an attractive texture.

Ribbon can also be used to hang glass jars filled with
flowers. Choose a jar with a neck and a slight lip around
the top. Knot one length of ribbon tightly around the
neck and tie the ends into a bow. With a second length
of ribbon make a 'handle' by which to hang the jar.

above left A striped silk bow trims a potted plant.
above right This flower-filled glass jar is hung like a
lantern by a length of plain ribbon and decoratively finished
with a patterned jacquard ribbon tied into a bow.

types of ribbon

There is an astonishing choice of ribbon colour, texture, pattern and width – varying from 1.5 mm (¹⁄₁₆ in) to 15 cm (6 in) – and each ribbon type has its most appropriate uses. For example, a hard-wearing washable and colourfast ribbon should be used if it is to be subjected to wear and tear, while more delicate ribbons are better suited for decorative purposes. The following ribbons are those most used in this book.

Satin and taffeta Satin ribbons are available as either single face (shiny on one side and matt on the other) or double face (shiny on both sides). They are available in single colours as well as patterns, and may be finished with a delicate picot edge. Taffeta, in contrast to satin, is nearly always matt and the same on both sides. It comes in plain colours, traditional plaids, checks and stripes. Ombré taffeta is colour shaded from one edge to the other, and moiré taffeta shimmers with a watermark. Both satin and taffeta ribbons are available with wire edges and with metallic trimmed edges.

Sheer ribbons, which include organdies and

ettes, are made from very finely woven yarns so

ht and delicate and appear almost translucent.

dies are often 'shot' – an effect produced by

g the ribbon in two contrasting colours so that it

es colour or appearance according to the way in

the light falls on it. Georgettes have a slightly matt appearance

se of their crepe texture. Sheer ribbons are often manufactured with a

woven or wire edge, which helps to give the fabric stability. They may

n or printed with delicate floral patterns, appliquéd or embroidered, or

orate a metallic thread. Sheer ribbons drape well and make the most

and romantic bows, particularly wreath bows (see page 98).

Jacquard These ribbons are woven, rather than printed,
with patterns ranging from the simplest of images to
highly elaborate designs involving many colours. The
weaving adds texture and creates a 'right' and a 'wrong'
side so that the ribbon is best used in a simple way
where the patterns can be seen and appreciated fully.

sgrain These ribbons have a distinctive

sways rib and are stronger and thicker to

le than most of the other ribbons. Grosgrain

traditionally used by milliners to decorate hats.

ribbon is available in solid colours, appliquéd,

erned – often striped – pleated and with picot edges.

Velvet This classic ribbon is woven with a distinctive plush
pile, usually on one side only. For this
reason it looks best when used in very
simple ways. Velvet ribbon is available in
various widths and can be found in
single colours, as well as with
printed or flocked patterns,
pleated and with a wire edge.
The fabric, particularly fine silk
velvets, should be treated with
care as the pile can be easily
crushed from repeated tying and
knotting. Dressmaking pins will also mark the
velvet so try to keep their use to a minimum.

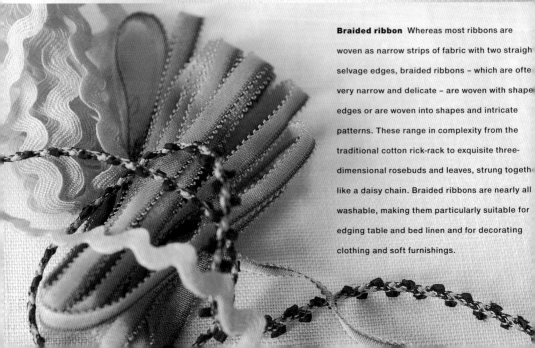

Braided ribbon Whereas most ribbons are
woven as narrow strips of fabric with two straigh
selvage edges, braided ribbons – which are ofte
very narrow and delicate – are woven with shape
edges or are woven into shapes and intricate
patterns. These range in complexity from the
traditional cotton rick-rack to exquisite three-
dimensional rosebuds and leaves, strung togeth
like a daisy chain. Braided ribbons are nearly all
washable, making them particularly suitable for
edging table and bed linen and for decorating
clothing and soft furnishings.

tallics These ribbons are made from metallic

eads, either used alone or combined with other

res. They may also be

nted with metallic

tifs, which makes

m a popular

ice for fes-

e occasions.

Wire-edge ribbons Most fabric ribbons

are available with wire

edges – a fine

flexible wire woven

along both edges –

which helps the ribbon

hold its shape when made into

a bow, or which may be pulled to

gather the ribbon for a ruffled

effect. Most wire-edge ribbons

cannot be washed. The wire

can easily be removed if

a 'normal' ribbon

is required.

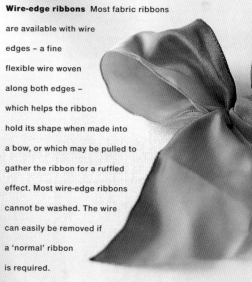

ated and frilled Most ribbon textures are available not only as flat

ric strips, but also come ready pleated, ruched

rilled. These techniques may have been

ked over the whole ribbon, for example a

ated taffeta or velvet, or along just one or

edges, as with a frill-edge satin

ruched gingham. Such

ons are not suitable

ying into elaborate

s but are best used

ly; they are ideal

dging soft

ishings: cushions,

shades and curtains.

single bow

This is the simplest bow of all and suitable for any type of ribbon. There is no twisting or complicate

looping so it is particularly suitable for ribbon with a 'right' and 'wrong' side, such as jacquard or

velvet, as well as heavier ribbon like grosgrain,

which is less versatile and difficult to knot well.

You will need 50 cm (20 in) of ribbon, plus a

short length of narrow ribbon or florist's wire.

one Lay the ribbon horizontally on a flat surface in front

of you. Overlap the two ends of the ribbon as shown.

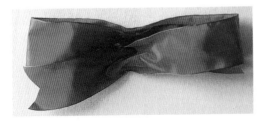

two Pinch the ribbon together in the centre, gather

up the fabric. **three** Tie the pinched centre with

narrow ribbon or florist's wire, knotting it at the back

the bow. Do not cut the excess ribbon or wire yet in case

it is needed to secure the bow to something. Puff out the

bow loops and twist the tails to point downward. If you

have not already done so, cut the ends of the ribbon

diagonally or in an inverted 'V' (see page 151).

double bow

You will need about 1.5 m (1¾ yd) of ribbon –
allowing more for a very wide ribbon – plus a
short length of narrow ribbon or florist's wire.

one Cut off a 50 cm (20 in) length of ribbon and put to
one side. On a flat surface arrange the remaining ribbon
coil with both ends of ribbon finishing opposite each other at roughly the same point, but slightly overlapping the
tre. Flatten the coil, keeping the ribbon ends near to the centre with the loops for the bow to either side. **two** Pinch
centre of the flattened coil and tie it with either narrow ribbon or florist's wire. Secure tightly at the back of the bow.

e To make the tails slide the reserved ribbon length

ar the bow and tie it around the centre, knotting it at

back. Fan out the bow loops and cut the tail ends

r diagonally or in an inverted 'V' (see page 151).

picture bow

Use one single ribbon or two contrasting ones.

You will need about 1 m (1¼ yd) of ribbon, plus

15.5 cm (6 in) of narrow ribbon or florist's wire.

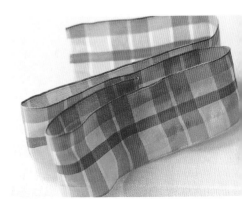

one Set aside a 40 cm (16 in) length of the ribbon and

arrange the remainder to make four loops as shown. Flat-

ten, making sure the ends of the ribbon are in a central

position but slightly overlapping the centre, with two loops arranged on either side. **two** Fold the reserved ribl

length in half and lay it under the flattened loops to make a cross, with the three loops of equal length. Place the nar

ribbon or wire under the vertical loop; bring both ends to the front to cross over in the centre. **three** Take the end

the back. Pull tightly to gather up the centre of the bow and knot to secure the loops and tails. Trim the loose e

four Gently puff out the bow and tails; cut the ends in an inverted 'V' (see page 151) if you have not already done

leated bow

is simple bow is ideal for ribbons that are

ficult to knot. You will need 56 cm (22 in) of

m (1½ in) wide ribbon, and 10 cm (4 in) of

.5 cm (1 in) wide contrasting ribbon.

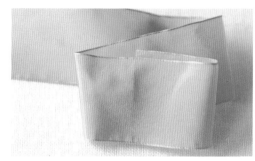

Place the longer length of ribbon horizontally on a

surface in front of you. Turn under 4 cm (1½ in) at the right-hand edge to form the first loop. Fold the ribbon again

8 cm (3 in) to form a second loop, returning the ribbon to the right, behind the first loop. **two** Repeat this folding

and looping, making the next two loops slightly wider

apart than the first two and the final two loops even more

so, to produce three sets of loops of increasing width –

the shortest to the front. The end of the ribbon should

finish in a central position in line with the beginning.

Secure the pleated ribbon with a staple in the

e. To finish the bow, wrap the shorter length of

around the centre to cover the staple and secure

back with either a dab of multi-purpose glue or

e-sided tape. Gently puff out the loops, if liked.

rosette bow

You will need 2.3 m (2½ yd) of a single wire-edge ribbon, or use contrasting colours or fabrics if like

one Cut a 60 cm (24 in) length of the wire-edge ribbon and lay it on a flat surface. Take one corner and pull 1

(⅜ in) of wire from the ribbon edge. Bend this end of wire back along itself to secure it. Take the end of the wire on

corresponding edge at the ot

end of the ribbon, and pull

gently so that the ribbon starts

ruffle and curl into a horses

shape. **two** As you continue to

the wire out with one hand, ge

tease the ruffles back towards

other end with your other hand. Keep pulling the wire until the length of ribbon is completely gathered. Cut the exc

wire, leaving a 2.5 cm (1 in) end to bend back along itself, as before, to secure the gathers. Fold under the last

(⅜ in) of the ribbon to hide the raw edge. Arrange the

gathered ribbon into a circle, overlapping the two ends

slightly and ensuring the neat turned-under edge is on

top. Using a needle, and thread to match the ribbon,

join the ends of the circle together with a few stitches.

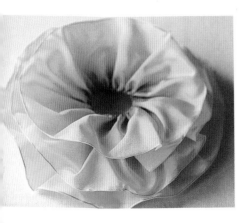
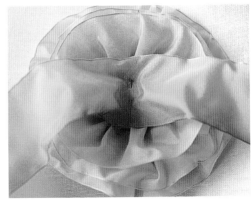

ree Cut 50 cm (20 in) of ribbon and repeat as for the first length of ribbon to make a slightly smaller gathered circle.

ke a third circle using 40 cm (16 in) of ribbon. To assemble the bow place the three gathered circles on top of each

er, the largest at the bottom and the smallest on top. **four** Place the circles on the object or surface you

h to decorate. Place

centre of the remain-

length of ribbon in the

dle of the circles. Pin

the object or surface beneath, or stick it using a dab

ulti-purpose glue – this will hold the circles in place.

Fold each tail end in half and cut at an angle to

e a perfectly symmetrical inverted 'V' at each end.

Tie the loose ends into a bow and pull the tails down.

acknowledgments

This book would not have been possible without the help and commitment of the following people. A very big thank you to Annabelle Lewis and everyone her wonderful shop, V V Rouleaux, for all their enthusiasm and enormous he I'd also like to thank Suki Dhanda, Claudia Dulak and Rosalind Fairman. I am indebted to Fiona Lindsay, my agent, for her guidance and encouragement, and to Jacqui Small who invited me to do this book. I'd also like to give a big thank you to everyone at Ryland Peters & Small, in particular Sally Powell, wh made sense of all the pictures and designed such a wonderful-looking book and Jo Lethaby, who so calmly brought order to the text.

In particular I wish to thank Sandra Lane who, in spite of the imminent arrival of Billy, took as always the most beautiful pictures. This book would not have been the same without her. Finally, a very special thank you to Charles, who is alway constant support and inspiration to me. **This book is dedicated to the 'flower girls' – Jenny, Gilly and Kath – with lo**

suppliers

The Berwick Street Cloth Shop
14 Berwick Street
London W1V 3RG
020 7287 2881
Good choice of fabrics.

Camden Passage Antiques Market
Islington Green
London N1
Wednesday and Saturday morning only. Old ribbons, fabrics and glass drops.

Columbia Road Flower Market
Columbia Road
London E2
Sunday morning only. Wreaths, dried exotic leaves, willow branches and shells.

The Conran Shop
81 Fulham Road
London SW3 6RB
020 7589 7401
Fabrics and table linen.

Heal's
196 Tottenham Court Road
London W1 P 9LD
020 7636 1666
www.heals.co.uk
Good for plain lampshades.

John Lewis
Oxford Street
London W1A 1EX
020 7629 7711
www.johnlewis.com
Ribbons, fabrics, lampshades and bed linen.

Liberty
210 Regent Street
London W1R 6AH
020 7734 1234
Ribbons and fabrics.

Neal Street East
Neal Street
Covent Garden
London WC2
020 7240 0135
Good choice of shells.

Paperchase
213 Tottenham Court Road
London W1P 7PS
020 7580 8496
Paper, card, glue, spray paints.

Selfridges
400 Oxford Street
London W1A 1AB
020 7629 1234
www.selfridges.co.uk
Table linen, china and glas

Bryony Thomasson
19 Ackmar Road
Parsons Green
London SW6 4UP
020 7731 3693
By appointment only. Spec in antique rustic textiles.

VV Rouleaux
54 Sloane Square
London SW1W 8AX
020 7730 3125
The ultimate shop for ribbo